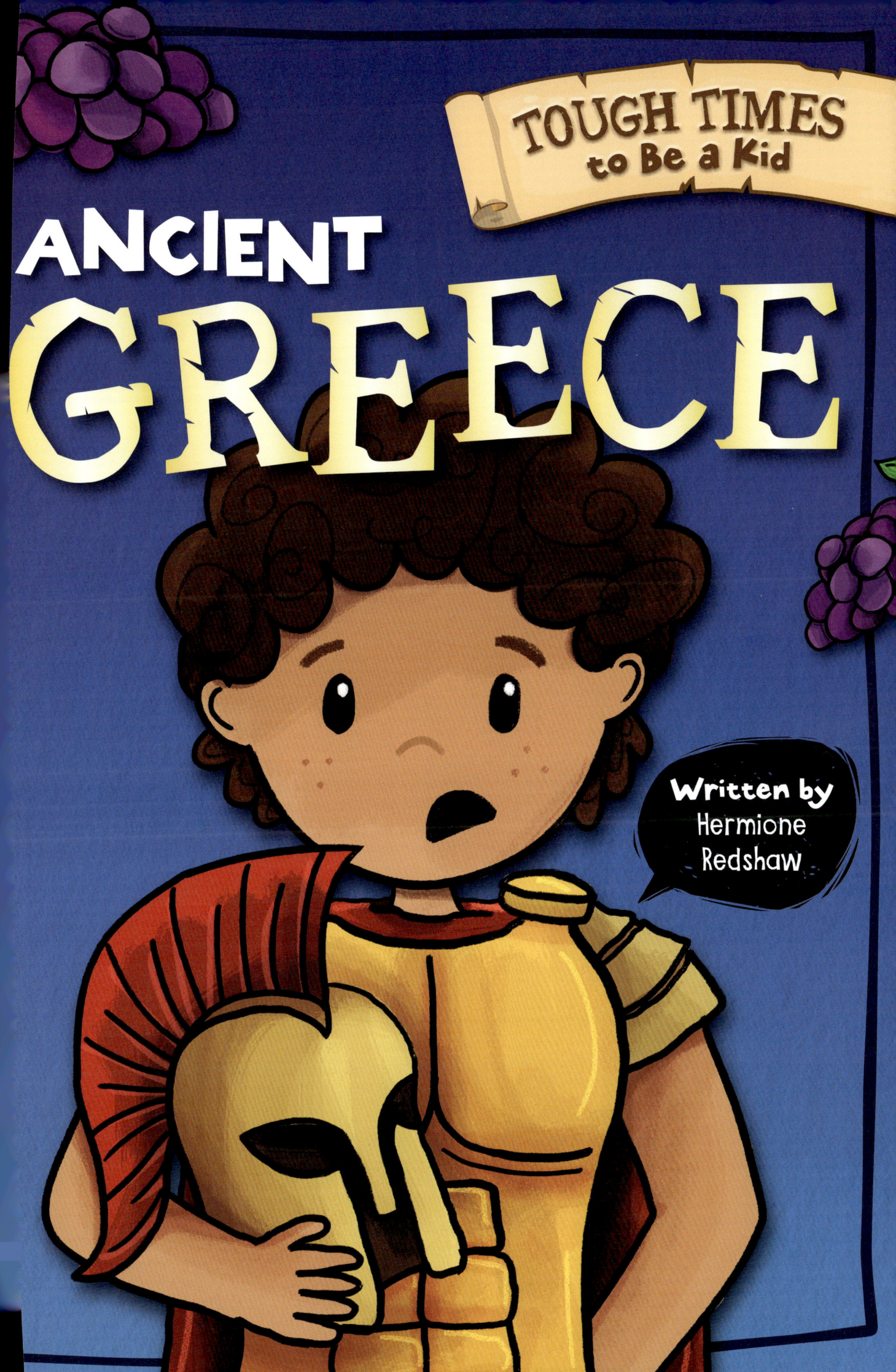

BookLife
PUBLISHING

©2023
BookLife Publishing Ltd.
King's Lynn, Norfolk
PE30 4LS, UK

All rights reserved.
Printed in Poland.

A catalogue record for this book is available from the British Library.

ISBN: 978-1-80155-848-8

Written by:
Hermione Redshaw

Edited by:
Robin Twiddy

Designed and illustrated by:
Amy Li

All facts, statistics, web addresses and URLs in this book were verified as valid and accurate at time of writing. No responsibility for any changes to external websites or references can be accepted by either the author or publisher.

CONTENTS

Page 4   Being a Kid
Page 6   Ancient Greece
Page 8   Surviving the Time
Page 10   Family Fun... but Where's Dad?
Page 12   Home Sweet Mud Home
Page 14   Don't Mess with the Gods!
Page 16   Honey, I'm Hungry
Page 18   What to Wear?
Page 20   Fun and Bones
Page 22   School of War
Page 26   Grown Up at What Age?
Page 30   That's Tough!
Page 31   Glossary
Page 32   Index

Words that look like this are explained in the glossary on page 31.

Being a KID

Being a kid is tough. School is boring, your tablet is always running out of charge and annoying parents stop you eating sweets all day. What's not tough about that?

What could be worse than HOMEWORK?

Imagine you live in a time where there is no sugar, no electricity and school only teaches you how to read and write. Now, you have just imagined what it's like to live in ancient Greece!

If you think being a kid is tough today, you had better prepare yourself. Ancient Greece really was a tough time to be a kid. Don't be fooled into thinking otherwise.

ANCIENT GREECE

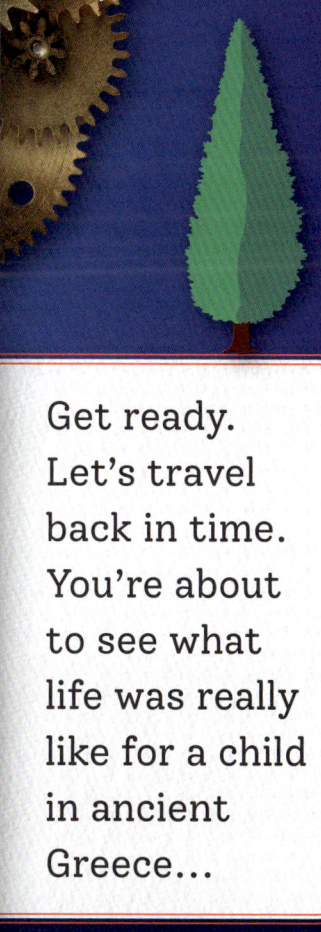

Get ready. Let's travel back in time. You're about to see what life was really like for a child in ancient Greece...

Ancient GREECE

Ancient Greeks lived over 3,000 years ago, between 800 BC and 31 BC. Their civilisation did not just include Greece as we know it today. It stretched into Europe, Egypt and part of Asia.

Some of the fun things we have today came from as far back as ancient Greece, such as theatre. Ancient Greece is also the reason we have the Olympic Games. The Greek Olympics was a sporting event in the city of Olympia that celebrated the god Zeus.

Zeus, God of Thunder

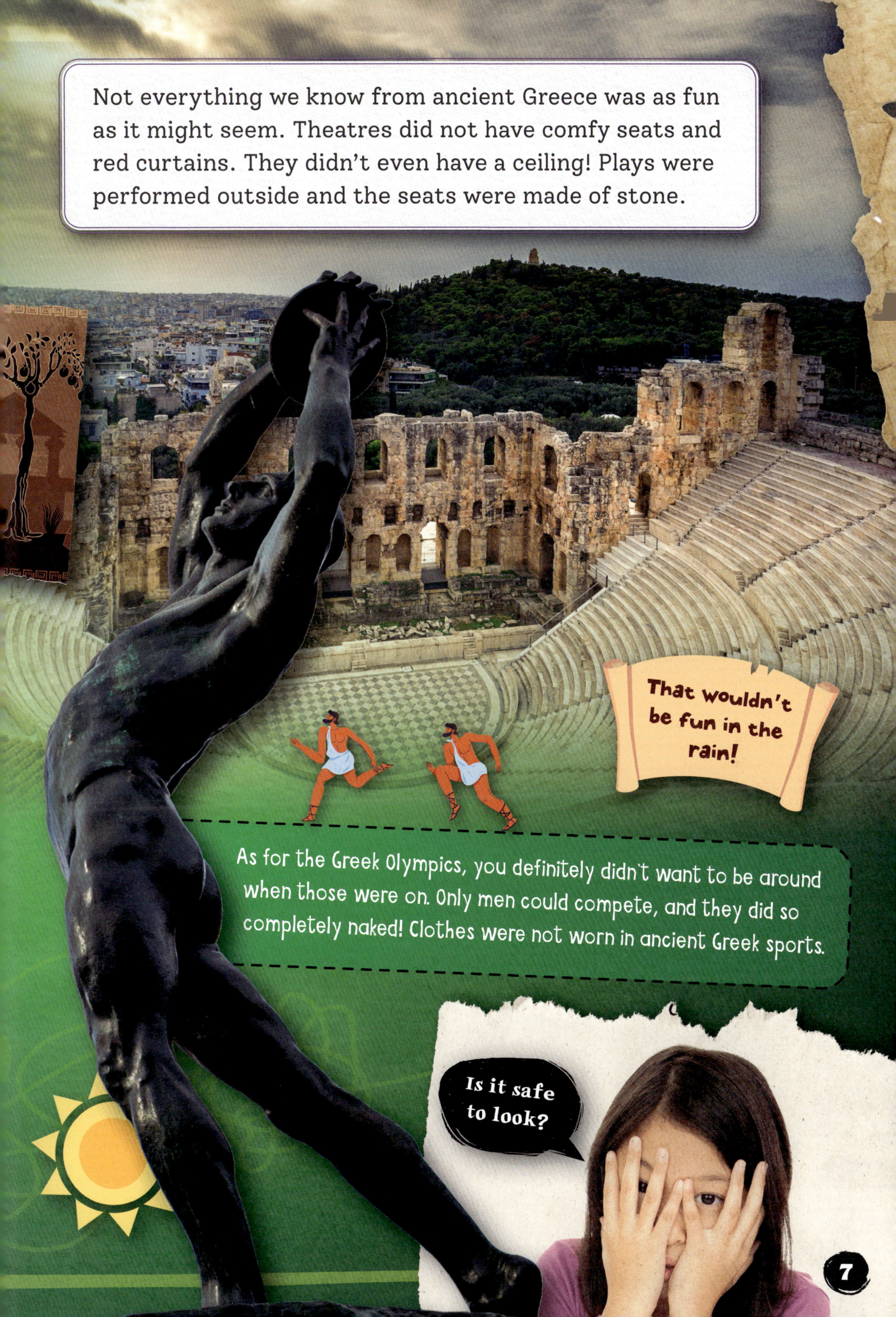

Not everything we know from ancient Greece was as fun as it might seem. Theatres did not have comfy seats and red curtains. They didn't even have a ceiling! Plays were performed outside and the seats were made of stone.

That wouldn't be fun in the rain!

As for the Greek Olympics, you definitely didn't want to be around when those were on. Only men could compete, and they did so completely naked! Clothes were not worn in ancient Greek sports.

Is it safe to look?

SURVIVING the Time

To know what it was like to be a kid in ancient Greece, you would first need to live long enough. That was tougher than you might think! Many babies would die before they reached one year old. Things that babies would survive today might have meant the end for them in ancient Greece.

What was that about babies?

First, ancient Greek babies had to survive their birth, which many mothers couldn't even survive at that time. Doctors and midwives did not have the same medicine or technology they have today. Most parents simply prayed to the gods for a safe birth.

If you survived your own birth, great!
Don't think you're out of the woods yet, though. Young children could easily become ill or catch diseases, and there were lots of diseases in ancient Greece! There were no vaccines to stop them, either.

Some of the 'cures' for illness in ancient Greece were as bad as the illness themselves. Doctors believed that having too much or too little of the liquids in your body could make you ill. They might take blood out of you to cure a pain in your side!

You're not taking MY blood!

FAMILY FUN
...But Where's Dad?

Families were a little bit different in ancient Greece. Your job as a kid might not have been to do well in school and tidy your room. However, for the time they were kids, ancient Greek children still got to act like children. That sounds fun... right?

Yeah, I'm just like you... I wish!

Just because children were allowed to play games and have fun at times, that doesn't mean family life was always easy for them. Far from it, in fact! Just how bad it could get might also depend on if you were poor or rich.

Rich or poor, don't expect to spend time with your dad. When men in ancient Greece weren't working, they ate meals or went places with their male friends, not their families. Men in the army might not see their wife and kids for years!

My family have probably forgotten who I am!

Me too!

Same here!

Sounds about right.

Being a kid is so TOUGH!

You and me both.

Ancient Greek mums were in charge of the home. They had to take care of the children, cook and clean. They also had to make clothes for everyone and collect water. It sounds tough to be a mum, too...

HOME Sweet Mud Home

Ancient Greek homes were often made from wood and mud bricks. They didn't have much furniture inside, and poor homes might not have any decoration or paint to hide those muddy walls.

Almost as soon as it got dark, most ancient Greeks went to bed. That meant early bedtimes in winter! There was no electricity back then, so the only light at night came from candles or oil lamps. Days inside might be just as dark as night, as there was no glass in windows, either. Wooden shutters were used to keep out the hot sun.

I wish my home wasn't so dark and muddy...

If you're planning on heading to bed for a good night's sleep, you might want to think again. Most families would sleep in the same room at night. Ancient Greek families could get large, too! You might find yourself squashed in a bed with your brothers, sisters, parents and grandparents!

Disgustingly, using the toilet was a social part of the day. Homes did not have running water, let alone a bathroom! People could use a public bathroom, or more often they would wash from a bucket or stream. As for ancient Greek toilets, they were just stone benches with holes in them!

Don't Mess With THE GODS!

The ancient Greeks were very religious people. They believed that many gods and goddesses helped to create the world as we know it. The gods also had a say over how things happened in the present. You did not want to mess with an ancient Greek god!

Did you know they also called me Zeus, King of the Gods? I can do much worse than just make thunder!

Did you ever hear about Sisyphus? The gods made him push a large boulder up a hill over and over again, forever! How about Medusa? The goddess Athena turned her hair into snakes! Good luck brushing that hair! There are many more stories like this from Greek mythology. In ancient Greece, mythology and religion were hard to tell apart.

Am I having a bad hair day?

Yesssss.

If something bad happened, it was probably because the gods were unhappy with you. Imagine being punished by a parent for doing something wrong. Well, it was probably ten times worse to get punished by a god.

Good luck working out which one is upset. There was a god for everything!

Do you think they'll find us up here?

To keep the gods on your side, you would need to pray to shrines or statues of gods. You might also leave presents for them or make sacrifices. Children sometimes helped to make animal sacrifices to the gods! How horrible!

Honey, I'M HUNGRY

Meat was not common to eat amongst the ancient Greeks. It was expensive to buy, meaning only the rich could afford to eat meat often. Even then, you wouldn't get a beef burger. You would have to make do with the hare, deer and wild boar on your plate.

I'd rather you didn't eat me, either!

You might also be fed octopus.

Many meals in ancient Greece involved fruits, vegetables and grains, such as bread. Eating all that horrible stuff didn't get rewarded, though. There was no sugar back then. Honey was used to sweeten things, meaning cakes would have tasted very different. Worst of all... there were no such things as sweets or chocolate!

Dionysus, God of Wine

No, thank you.

Water was not always clean in ancient Greece. Milk was mostly for the rich. So, what did people drink? The main drink was wine. Yuck! They even had a god for it! While that might have been all right for grown-ups, it sounds like kids had a tough time finding something to drink.

Rich or poor, there were no knives and forks. Everyone ate with their fingers. Food was often cut up in the kitchen to make it easier to eat like this. However, it still was not as easy as we have it today... and it was definitely messier!

What to WEAR?

Ancient Greek costumes are great for a fancy dress party. However, the clothes you might find for dressing up aren't exactly what real ancient Greek children would have worn.

Thank the gods we didn't have the Winter Olympics!

So, what did they wear? The answer is not very much! Young children might have worn a short piece of cloth tied around their middle. However, they more often wore nothing at all, especially if they were playing a sport.

"This is much better than thin cloth!"

"It still is..."

Once you were old enough to start wearing clothes, you might wear a tunic. Yes, that thin piece of cloth like a sheet was about all you would wear. Male tunics went down to their knees, while female tunics went down to their feet.

Poor people might even have tunics made from actual sheets!

Just like today, hair fashion changed throughout ancient Greece. Whatever the style, statues often showed ancient Greeks with curls. Of course, not everyone has curly hair, so how did they hold the curls in place? Well, they used beeswax!

FUN and BONES

Ancient Greek children had toys, just like kids today. They had dolls, balls and marbles to play with. Things like yo-yos and hobby horses haven't changed much over the years. However, the rest might surprise you.

Would you rather play video games or a game with small stones like marbles? Well, children in ancient Greece didn't have video games. They didn't really have marbles, either. They used small bones from animals, known as 'knucklebones'.

Bones for toys?!

Those kids just invited me to play ball with them!

At least a ball to play with doesn't sound too weird. Well, until you find out what it was made from. If you were lucky, a ball might be a bunch of tied up rags. Otherwise, it would be a pig's bladder filled with air.

By now, you may have guessed that dolls weren't any better in ancient Greece. Dolls were made from all sorts of strange materials. Some were even made from clay, wax or glass!

Careful not to hug your toys too tight! They might break!

Ancient Greek dolls

SCHOOL of War

Children would go to school from the ages of 7 to 14. That's hardly any time at all compared to schools today. However, don't go celebrating just yet. Ancient Greek schools were tough.

Only the rich could afford to send their children to a proper school. Those who could not afford it might be taught by a parent, and they might be the lucky ones. Kids had to do their homework on two wax tablets tied together with string. That's a heavy book for your school bag!

Education was different for boys and girls. Boys would learn how to be a good citizen in order to take part in public life when they were older. Let's hope you're good at public speaking! Meanwhile, girls had it really tough. They were only taught how to cook, clean and look after a family.

I'd rather be at school than clean every day.

Most children would learn to read, write and do simple maths. Poor boys might learn how to take over their father's job. You may spend your school days cleaning up a farm. Otherwise, you could end up in military school. Maths probably doesn't sound so bad now.

23

THE SPARTAN ARMY

Why did my parents have to move us to Sparta?

Some boys might not even get to school at all if they lived in a place called Sparta. In Sparta, children belonged to the state rather than their parents. These children were raised to be soldiers.

I'm not weak, I promise!

When a baby was born in Sparta, it would be carefully examined to see if it was strong. If the baby was weak, it might be abandoned on a hillside.

"We're Spartan! It can't be that tough... can it?"

At age seven, boys would be taken from their homes to join the Spartan army. Being a Spartan boy was tough because Spartans had to be tough. They would be put through some very harsh things to make them strong.

"OUCH! OW! I miss my sandals!"

The boys would have to march without shoes and go without food. They learnt how to fight and how to handle pain. There would be no breaks, either! You didn't even get to sleep in your own home at the end of each long day.

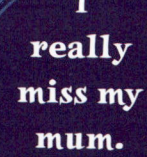

"I really miss my mum."

Spartan boys lived away from home as Spartans believed that having a mother around would make them weak.

GROWN UP
at WHAT age?

There were no teenagers in ancient Greece. Once you were done being a child, you skipped straight ahead to being treated like an adult. Finally! No one to tell you to tidy your room or do your homework. You can do whatever you want.

Unfortunately, being an adult was not so easy, either. Girls became adults at around 12 years old. They would often be seen as adults before boys. However, now that they were classed as women, it would be time to get married.

I'M NOT READY TO GET MARRIED!

Marriages in ancient Greece were often sorted by the girl's father or a male relative. Girls did not get a say in who their husbands would be. The bride and groom might not even meet until the wedding.

Oh, so you're my new husband?

Say goodbye to all of your toys once you turn 12. As part of becoming a woman, girls had to give away their toys to the gods. What do the gods need with all those toys?

I don't care if you've had that teddy all your life. The gods want to play with it now!

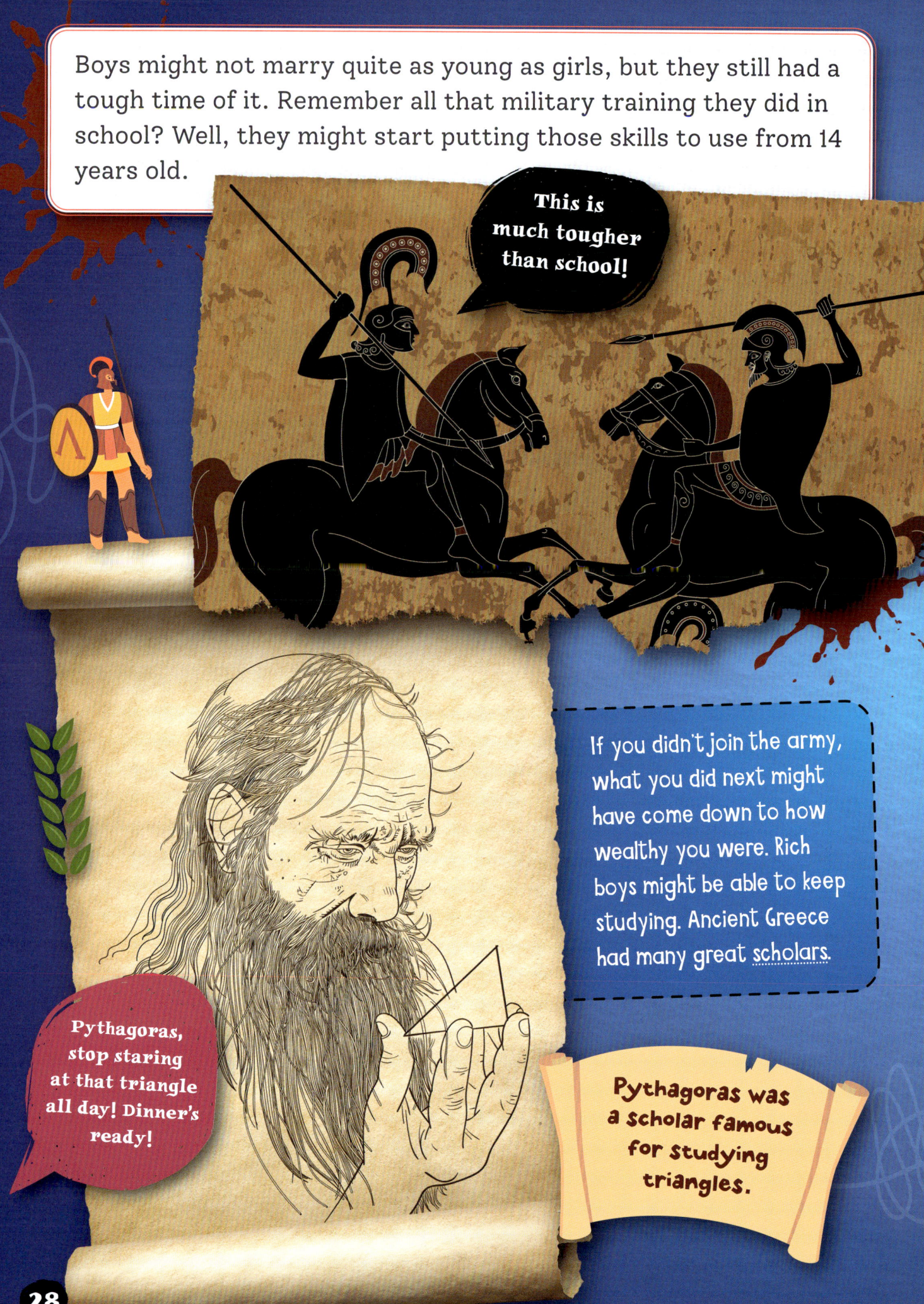

Boys might not marry quite as young as girls, but they still had a tough time of it. Remember all that military training they did in school? Well, they might start putting those skills to use from 14 years old.

This is much tougher than school!

If you didn't join the army, what you did next might have come down to how wealthy you were. Rich boys might be able to keep studying. Ancient Greece had many great scholars.

Pythagoras, stop staring at that triangle all day! Dinner's ready!

Pythagoras was a scholar famous for studying triangles.

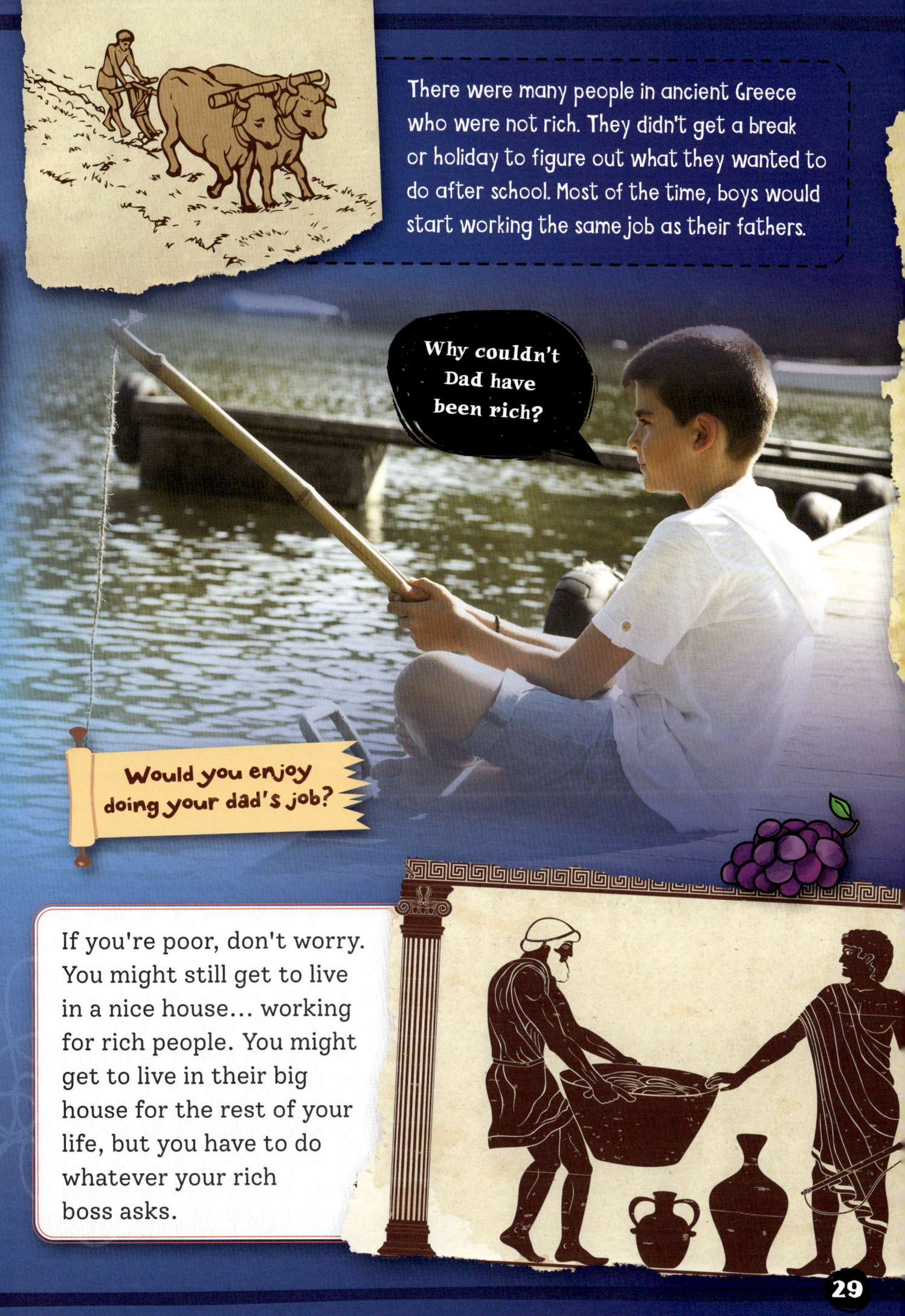

That's TOUGH!

Well, you thought being a kid was tough today. Thank goodness you don't live in ancient Greece! From mud houses to getting married at 12, ancient Greece was not a fun time to be a kid... and that's if you survived your childhood with all those diseases.

Don't worry, though. You can relax back into the present. You don't need to worry about getting married or joining the army. Now, let's get back to enjoying being a kid here and now.

Which part of life in ancient Greece would you struggle with the most?

GLOSSARY

BC	meaning 'before Christ', it is used to mark dates that occurred before the starting year of most calendars
bladder	a part of the body that gets bigger as it is filled and smaller as it empties
citizen	legally recognised member of a country or state
civilisation	a group of people and their way of living
diseases	illnesses that affect a person
electricity	something that is carried through wires and is used to make machines, lights and things work
liquids	something that can flow freely
materials	something from which something else is made
midwives	a person who helps a woman when she is giving birth
mythology	the traditional stories of a group that often explain the world around them and how it was formed
punished	made to suffer for doing something bad
relative	a member of the family
religious	believing in a god or group of gods and following the rules of a religion
sacrifices	to give up something important, sometimes the life of an animal or a loved object
scholars	people who have studied something for a long time and know lots about it
shrines	places connected with someone or something important to them, such as a god
social	spending time with other people
state	a group of people within a certain area
technology	a machine or piece of equipment that was created to solve problems
theatre	the art or activity of performing plays on a stage
vaccines	something that is injected into a person to protect against a disease

INDEX

armies 11, 25, 28, 30

babies 8, 24

books 22

doctors 8–9

dolls 20–21

knucklebones 20

meat 16

Olympics 6–7, 18

Pythagoras 28

Sparta 24–25

tablets 4, 22

tunics 19

wax 21–22

wine 17

Photo Credits All images are courtesy of Shutterstock.com, unless otherwise specified. With thanks to Getty Images, Thinkstock Photo and iStockphoto.

Recurring images – YamabikaY, Tartila, TADDEUS, sumkinn, Vlada Young, Gaidamashchuk, pics five, Andrey_Kuzmin, SurfsUp, SofiaV, DarthVector, dimethylorange, Milano M. Cover - Renata Sedmakova, Ikpro, Thanasis Foukas. 2-3 - Richard Panasevich. 4-5 - donatas1205, Lambros Kazan, rangizzz, Veja. 6-7 - Daniel Eskridge, Georgios Tsichlis, Liza888, matrioshka, Oligo22, RusskyMaverick. 8-9 - VikiVector, aelina_design, Andrey Levitin, Avihay Elharar, Eroshka, Gilmanshin. 10-11 - Maryna Kulchytska, Massimo Todaro, vkilikov. 12-13 - Demkat, Myurenn, N-studio, Panos Karas, pixels outloud, Sabphoto, Stefan Lambauer. 14-15 - Allik, delcarmat, markara, Rroselavy, Songquan Deng. 16-17 - Africa Studio, Anatoliy Karlyuk, dragi52, HalynaRom, Hoika Mikhail, Khosro, Tkachov Oleh. 18-19 - anat chant, ArtFamily, Gilmanshin, Siberian Art, U. Eisenlohr. 20-21 - Dorieo (Wikimedia Commons), Oscar Peralta Anechina, Perfect_kebab, Photo Oz, WH_Pics, yevgeniy11. 22-23 - Iryna Inshyna, Nataliia Maksymenko, Prostock-studio. 24-25 - AlyonaZhi, naya, Kaspars Grinvalds, Naty_Lee, NotionPic, Pavel_Markevych, Serhii Bobyk, tan_tan. 26-27 - Fenixx666, Giorgio G, matrioshka, Olga Zhukovskaya, ONYXprj, Sergei Kolesnikov. 28-29 - ArtMari, carballo, Hoika Mikhail, Naci Yavuz, tan_tan. 30 - Veja.